# I'*m Still Here, Lord!*

# I'm Still Here, Lord!

## BETTY ISLER

Concordia Publishing House
St. Louis

Library of Congress Catalog Data
Isler, Betty, 1915-
    I'm still here, Lord!

    1. Women—Prayer-books and devotions—English.
I. Title.
BV4844.I83   1984                    242'.643                    84-7018
ISBN 0-570-03938-X

1 2 3 4 5 6 7 8 9 1 0     CB     93 92 91 90 89 88 87 86 85 84

# Contents

# For All Eternity

Some things never change...
The moon, the stars,
The sun, the tides,
The mountains,
The seas...

Your love,
Your compassion,
Your forgiveness,
All of these...

Which is why
I'm still here, Lord,
On my knees.

# A Quiet Psalm

No ten-stringed instruments
Have I,
No harp or psaltery;
No timbrel, cymbal,
Flute, or lute
Accompany my days.

But deep within
The soul of me
A steady music plays,
My own unending song to Him
Of wonderment and praise.

# Repetition

Lord,
I must be a slow learner
That You need to teach me
This same lesson
Over and over:
To put my trust in You
COMPLETELY.

But one thing
Is solidly anchored
In my mind:
No matter how long
It may take me,
You will never
Forsake me.

# Introducing the Day

Lord,
Dawn came up
Over Saddleback this morning
With such a rush
That the colors spilled
Across the whole sky
And ran together,
All rosy and blurry.

I suppose You have
So many miracles
Scheduled for today
You had to get Your show
On the road
In a hurry.

# The Invisible Loom

This outer garment of faith
Which I so gladly wear
Is too often subjected,
Human as I am,
To every rip and tear
Of daily living.

I am so thankful
For that strong, inner lining
Which clings beneath . . .
That sturdy fabric
Of belief,
Which the Spirit
Is constantly
Reweaving.

# Evening Confession

Lord,
This has been a day
Of things gone wrong,
Maddening frustrations,
Petty irritations.

I have been cross
And petulant,
Totally out of touch
With my family,
The whole tone of the day
Off key and out of balance
Because I upset it.

Lord,
Please forgive me
These past hours
And erase them
From my record.
If the day went wrong,
It is because
I let it.

# Off Ramp

Lord,
Sometimes I think
One of heaven's greatest joys
Must be the absence
Of gasoline fumes
And traffic noise.

Leaving the freeway,
With my head ringing
From fast-lane pressure,
I think of Your
Far pavilions,
So sunny and serene,
With only the tiniest birdsong
To ripple that clean
And healing air.

How quiet it must be!
I am sure You
Would never allow
Trucks and autos there.

# Bank Account

Lord,
In matters of arithmetic
I always come up short.
A balanced checkbook
Is a rarity for me.

Which makes me
More than ever grateful
For my long-standing account
With You,
Where my checks never bounce
And my balance is never overdrawn
Even when my deposits
Are so shamefully few.

# Urban Renewal

Lord,
She does not want to move,
But civic authorities have zoned
Her property for a
Brittle new mall.

They do not understand
That this old house
Fits her like
A warm, comfortable shawl.

They are rocking her boat,
Forcing her into
Strange waters
And onto an alien shore.

Lord,
As You have before,
Reach down Your hand
To this frail mother
And help her across
This Jordan
To her new land.

# Job Application

Lord,
I come to You
With a worksheet
That does me no credit.
My time schedule
Is erratic,
I've often been tardy,
Frequently absent.

Yet You do not even look
At my resumé…
Do not ask for any reference,
Seem not to care
About past experience.
Mercifully,
You just say
"Come."

# His Country

Lord,
I am continually impressed
By the fact that
You set no limits upon us.

You never say,
"I will go with you this far,
But no farther."
You never say,
"I will help you this much,
But no more."
You never say,
I will forgive you this time,
But not again!"

In the vast acres of
Your immeasurable love
And infinite patience,
There are no boundaries,
And no fences.

# Morning Prayer

Lord,
Once again You have given me
Another bright and wonderful day,
Lovingly gift-wrapped
And full of promised blessings.

Grant me the wisdom
Not to fritter it away.
Let me spend the hours
In ways pleasing to You.
Let me carefully use them
And not abuse them.

# Kinship

Lord,
I feel comfortable
Talking to You
In my own kind
Of crazy mental shorthand.
I never have to repeat
Or explain anything.
You always understand.

I never have to back up
And start over again
Or apologize
Or make amends.

I guess that is because
You and I
Are such close,
Personal friends.

# Grandmother at Communion

Her knees
No longer bend
As they once did,
And so she must stand
To receive the Bread
And the Cup.

But her heart
Kneels before her Lord,
Even while
She is standing up.

# Vacation Packing

I have been known
To forget essentials
Like toothpaste
And road maps,
Have even gone off
Without my glasses
Or campground passes,
And neglected to check
For dripping taps.

But Lord,
One thing
I never forget to do:
I never, never
Leave home without
You!

# Questions

Lord,
I lament, with Paul,
The things I do
And the things
I do not.
I make no excuse,
For I have none.

But Lord,
Sometimes I wonder
If this failing
Is not a part of
The human condition
Common to everyone,

Reminding us
Each day anew
Of our debt
To You.

# Words Unspoken

The woman who lived
Across from me
Would come and go
So quietly.

She seemed so distant
And kept to her own.
I shrugged my shoulders
And left her alone.

But Lord,
Last night she took her life,
Driven by demons
Of inner strife
That we, her neighbors,
Could not know,
And I, who never said "Hello"
Am sick with shame
And guilt that I
Now cannot even say
"Good-bye."

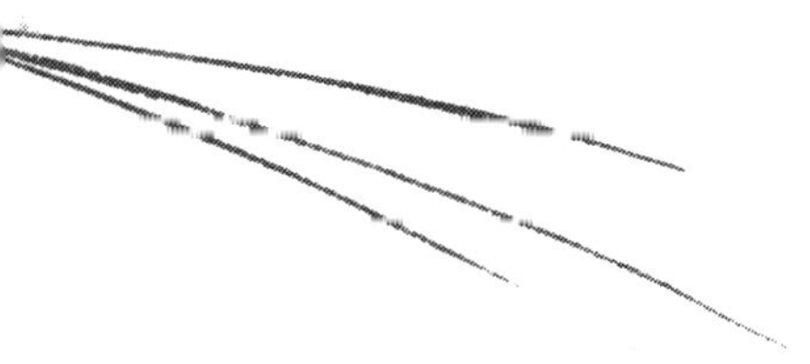

# Sticks and Stones

Lord,
Please help me to develop
What is called a thick skin.

Not so tough
That I become insensitive
To the feelings of others,
But sturdy enough
To withstand a few
Brickbats and criticisms.

I am too easily hurt
By what others
Think or say or do.

Help me to remember
All that really matters
Is how I rate
With You.

26

# Evaluation

Lord,
You know well enough
I am a disorganized person.
A teacher once told me
I had poor work habits.
(She should see me now!)

There are times
When my house requires
Not so much a vacuum
As a plow.
My kitchen should be posted
"Enter at Your Own Risk,"
And I am frankly ashamed
Of the top of my desk.

Sometimes my husband
Can find me only by
Following the path of crumbs
Which I leave like
Gretel and Hansel.

So Lord,
I shall try to be neater.
I will start by making
A list of things to do . . .

As soon as I find
My pencil.

# Relaxation

At the beach
Lying on the warm,
Receiving sand,
I feel my taut muscles
Loosen and relax.

The waves, washing ceaselessly
In and out
Lull me into a
Trancelike peace,
Muffling the
Squeals and shouts
Of prancing children
Busy with sand buckets,
Brown feet dancing,
Never still.

Seagulls strut awkwardly
On matchstick legs
At the water's edge,
Then lift with
Surprising grace,
Wings arched against that
Gloriously uncluttered
Blue space
As they float away.

Thank You, Lord,
For the healing magic
Of a perfect beach day

## *First Noel*

Of all church music
Through the year
The sweetest must be
The children's Christmas choir,
Offered so cheerfully
By that group of
Scrubbed and shining
Norman Rockwell cherubs,
Their innocent faces beaming
Above the white collars
As they sing their hearts out
In voices so earnest
And clear.

I fall in love with them
All over again
Each time they appear,
Caroling Your praises,
So refreshing and sincere.

# Slow Me Down, Lord

This woman,
Whom I admire so much,
Goes about Your work
In such a quiet,
Low-key manner,
Accomplishing in her steady,
Unbroken pace,
A hundred times more than I,
Who seem often to be
Running in place.

She serves you so well
With her unhurried poise,
Day after day,
While I tear around
Pell-mell.

I wish I had
Her way.

# Instant Communication

It is comforting to have
The little round sticker
On the telephone dial
Giving the number to call
In an emergency.

I am even more reassured
When I don't have to remember
An area code or even
Dial nine eleven
To reach heaven.

## Insight

Lord,
I am learning
That when I belittle myself,
As I frequently do,
I am also belittling You,
Who have made me
In Your own image!

Certainly I have faults
And shortcomings,
You know them all,
But perhaps these loud
Self-accusations
Ring somehow false
And out of place.

I think now that
One who would reflect
Your grace
Does so quietly.

# Laying Up Treasure

We pour over bank leaflets,
Discussing the merits
Of trust fund
Or money market accounts,
Trying to decide
Which pays the highest interest
And is the most
Economical.

Lord,
We are much better off
Putting our trust in You,
And Your interest rates
Are truly astronomical!

# The Stay-at-Home

Lord,
There is so much
I have not done.

I have never been
Hang gliding;
Have never ridden
A camel
Or been shot
From a cannon.
Have not been on a
Jungle safari,
Or climbed Mount Everest.

Now that I think of it,
I have not even been
To Philadelphia to see
The Liberty Bell.

But Lord,
In this uneventful,
Prosaic life of mine,
I hope I have spent
My time well
In doing the one thing
Needful to do...
Serving You.

# One Peaceful Summer Day

We packed a picnic lunch
And took the back roads
Up into the foothills,
Past the shaggy ranks of eucalyptus
Lining the orange groves.

We parked in the wide shade
Of a great live oak,
It's tiny leaves
Rustling their welcome,
And spread the cloth
On the cool earth.
I had forgotten the salt,
But the good country air
Carried its own spice.

We ate in comfortable silence,
Feeling the tensions of the week
Slowly fall away.
I fed the last of the cake crumbs
To a greedy jay.
My husband leaned back
Against the solid tree trunk,
Gave a sigh, and said,
"This is nice."

It was more than nice, Lord.
It was a keepsake kind of day,
A ruby, to be set apart
In the treasure box
Of the heart.

## Fitness Witness

The therapist wants
Too much of me,
To bend my head
And touch my knee.
"Impossible!" I say,
Half crying.
"These poor, stiff bones
Can never make it!"
But she insists
The benefit comes
From trying and trying.

Lord,
Is that not
The heart of Your teaching?
To live our lives
As You would have us,
Is always a matter
Of stretching and reaching.

## "I" Witness

I was not there at Bethlehem
To wait Your humble birth.
I did not walk with You those miles
You trod upon this earth;

Nor was I one to drink the wine
As Cana's wedding guest.
I did not stand beneath the cross
At darkest Calvary;

But surely as the world revolves,
To this I can attest:
I did not see, and yet I know
You lived and died for me!

# The Trail Blazer

Nothing can hurt so much
That You have not
Suffered more;

No tears that sorrow
Can bring
That You have not known
Their sting;

No path so rocky
Or perilous
That You have not
Traveled before.

# Now

When I wept,
I knew Your comfort.
When I suffered,
I felt Your healing.
When I weakened,
You gave me strength,
And when I anguished
You eased my stress;

But until I forgave another
I had not really known
The depth, the width,
The breadth, the vastness
Of Your own forgiveness.

## Counting to Ten

Lord,
Today I let people
Get under my skin
And irritate me.
They turned me off.
My patience is gone again!

O Lord!
Help me to remember
It is I who sin.
Help me to turn
The other cheek
And let Your love
Turn me on again.

# Let My Light So Shine

I have not seen a firefly
Since I was a child,
But I remember marveling
How such a dull,
Daytime creature
Could somehow produce
That glowing evening light.

Lord,
Is that not how
You sometimes use humans,
Placing Your flame
In the least of us,
Where it remains,
Always burning but
More noticeable
On a troubled night?

# Flight Pattern

Lord,
Another thing I have found
(I learn something new
Every day!)
Is that traveling with You
Is First Class
All the way.

## Weighing In

Lord,
Let me be proud
To serve You
But humble
Before You.

Let me be strong
In convictions,
But gentle
In manner.

Let me be loud
In Your praise
But soft-spoken
In prayer.

Lord,
Between assertion
And humility,
Strike Your balance
In me.

# The Watchman

Lord,
I am so weary.
Fatigue is my fellow traveler,
And I walk with lead
In my shoes.
I have pushed myself
To finish this task,
And now I feel spent,
Battered and bruised.
My bones threaten
To collapse into a heap
And all I want to do
Is sleep.

So Lord,
Here is the key
To my humble nest.
Please take care of things
While I rest.

# Post Surgery

Lord,
I have been down
This road before.
The landmarks are familiar,
The steep hills,
The discouraging slips,
The stumbling,
The dips.

Yes, I know this road,
But I could still
Lose my way
If You did not lead me
Night and day.

# Member of the Cast

Lord,
I do not like the limelight.
In a group of people
I prefer to drift
Into the background.
I am uncomfortable
On stage, or at the
Center of things.

If it is all right
With You, Lord,
I would rather serve You
From the wings.

# Prescription

Lord,
I have been put
Through the paces,
Having been prodded,
Poked, pushed, and
Peered at clinically,
And pronounced fit.

"Fit for what?" I ask,
Cynically,
As I climb down
Off their diagnostic
Assembly line,
Still weary and
Heavy laden.

Then I hear Your reply:
"Child, only I
Can look into Your soul.
Come Unto Me!"

# Beneath the Surface

Lord,
This woman,
Whom I long to reach,
Wears an invisible armor
About her.

Words cannot dent it,
Or warmth melt it.
Friendly gestures
Barely touch the surface
And glance off it.
I think she needs help,
But cannot show it.

Lord,
Help me to cut through
Her resistance
With the laser beam
Of Your love,
So she may know it!

# There Is Hope

Lord,
I think I am finally
Making progress.

Today in our group
There was disagreement,
A clashing of personalities,
And I felt anger
Building in me
For a minute.

But would You believe
I held my tongue,
Kept my peace,
Submerged the anger
And, wonder of wonders,
Felt love take
Its place?

Thank You, Lord,
For this small step
Forward for me.
I know Your will
Was in it.

# Tribulations

This path lately
Has been very rocky,
Uneven and crumbling
At the edges.
I go about stumbling
And unsteady.
I seem to have lost
The rhythm to my life,
My steps are
Out of cadence.

What keeps me going
Is knowing
That around every bend
Waits Jesus,
My friend.

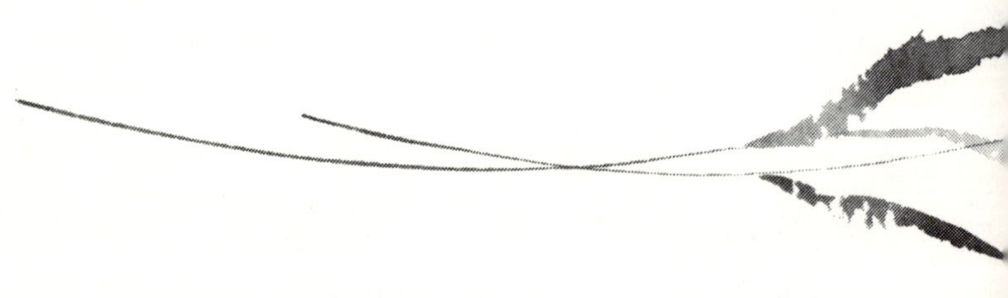

# Hunger

Merchandisers really provoke me
When they package their product
In multiples, so that
When I want one
I have to buy at least three.
I never know what to do
With the rest of the stuff.

But when it comes
To Your word, Lord,
That is another story.
No matter how it is packaged,
I can never get enough!

# Let Us Adore

Lord,
I have always felt
So close to you
In the out-of-doors,
In the awesome setting
Of mountaintop,
On the desert,
Or beside the sea.

But I also draw strength
From the formal ritual
Of Sunday service
Within Your house.
I love the royal colors
Of the banners
As they are marched
Down the aisle.
I love the golden glow
Of altar candelabra,
The rustle of vestments,
The dramatic organ music.
I feel supported by
The structure of
Ancient liturgy.

It seems wherever
We worship You
There is both simplicity
And majesty.

## Reward

Every now and then
A star falls in my path
Of one kind or another.

Today in a department store
I came upon a little lost boy,
Weeping and frightened.
He put his small
Birdlike hand in mine,
And I helped him find
His mother.

# Letter from Home

Her handwriting
Is so spidery now
And her lines
Run downhill.
It is hard for her
To hold the pen
But the spelling
Is correct.
She always prided herself
On such.
She gives a thimbleful
Of news, just enough
To keep in touch
And closes with
"God bless you, dear."

Lord,
Keep her guardian angel near.

# Free for the Taking

The world seems to have
An obsession for security,
Brought on by mankind's
Shameful faults...

Padlocks, night chains,
Burglar alarms,
Guard dogs,
Hidden safes,
Steel vaults...

How merciful, Lord,
That our most precious possession,
Your Word, need never be
Under lock and key.

# Right Place, Right Time

Lord,
There are so many situations
I must face
Where I find myself
Too early, or too late,
On the other side
Of the street,
Or in the wrong place.

But Lord,
Whatever should betide me,
You are always there...
Not before me,
Not behind me,
But beside me.

# The Lady in Room 401

She is such a small,
Brown sparrow of a woman,
So delicate and frail
A loud whisper
Could blow her away.
Yet she sits
In her wheelchair
Day after day,
Sharing Your love,
Telling of Your
Goodness and mercy,
Spreading Your Word
To those around her,
Upholding other patients
With the strength
Of an eagle.

# Final Arbitration

Lord,
With this good man,
In this good marriage,
I cannot pretend that
We never quarrel.

We do.

We are sometimes
At an impasse...
His will against mine
Until each gives in
To a greater will...
Thine.

# Retreat

This patio is my sanctuary
On summer mornings.
I come out early,
Before anyone is stirring.
Everything is still
And all the ferns hold
Dewdrops at their tips.
Only the hummingbird,
His tiny wings whirring,
Breaks the quiet
While he sips
At the feeder.

I like to have my own
Private time with You,
Before the day intrudes,
Before all the small,
Mechanical processes
Of living grind
Into gear.

You seem to sit next to me
Out here.
Can I get You
A cup of coffee,
Lord?

## Quandary

Lord,
I got myself
Into this mess,
And now I am asking You
To get me out of it.

I acted hastily,
Impulsively, and now
I am in a position
Too embarrassing
To mention.

Speak to me again, Lord.
This time I'm paying
Attention!

# Teenage Disciple

At the market
I am delighted to see
That the carryout boy
Wears a button that says
"I Love Jesus."

He is so enthusiastic
And his grin so
Joyous and unabashed
That I can forgive him
When I get home
And find all the tomatoes
Smashed!

# November Selections

The voting booth
Is too small,
The ballot too large,
The issues too complex
For a single
Yes or no answer.
And whom can we trust
To govern our affairs
In this political game?

Lord,
I keep a mental picture
Of a blank space
For a write-in vote,
Where I can place
Your name.

## Moving Day

Lord,
Just exactly what
Did You have in mind,
Giving me this
Gargantuan task
And a weak back?

Of course,
I should know better
Than to ask.
You always supply
The strength
I lack.

60

# Musical Score

Lord,
Some days are just better
Than others.
I never quite
Know why,
Except that I get up
Completely in tune
With You,
And everyone around me
And the day keeps on
Escalating.

I think the secret
Must be that
You are doing
The orchestrating.

# Young Woman in the Market

I could tell she had been
Crying all night.
Her face was a ravaged mask
Of grief and anguish
And her eyes, now dry,
Held no light.

Two unsmiling children
Clung to her skirts,
And it seemed to take
All her strength
To push the cart,
Loaded with groceries
And her burdens.

I was a stranger,
But I wanted to put
My arms around her
And tell her everything
Would be all right.
I wanted to tell her
Tomorrow would be better,
And turn her away
From whatever problems
Life had made for her.

But I was a stranger,
So I prayed for her.

## Calm Me Down, Lord

Lord,
When I plan a dinner
For a large number of guests
(Meaning more than two),
Why do I always
Fall apart
At the last minute
And let things
Go wrong?

After all,
I am not feeding
The five thousand,
But frankly, Lord,
I think I need
One of Your miracles
Almost as much
As that throng!

# Chef Pro Tem

Thank You, Lord,
For this good man of mine
Who so gleefully
Takes over the cooking
When I am not up to par.

He has his own methods,
Unorthodox by far,
And brings me strange meals
On unmatched china,
But how can I complain
When he is so cheerful
And willing to pitch in,
And even whistles
While he lays waste
To my kitchen?

# Into Your Care

I can still remember
The picture on a
Sunday school leaflet
That impressed me
Long ago.

It showed a carefree little girl
Running along a cliffside,
Unaware of any danger,
And above her there hovers
Your guardian angel.

I thought of it again
Last week, when
My little granddaughter
Went off to camp.

# From the Woman's Page

She drives a luxury car,
Has a palatial home,
Expensive jewelry,
Wears Paris-designed clothes,
Hobnobs with royalty,
And knows everyone
In the Social Register,
But she does not know
Her Lord.

What a poor,
Impoverished
Woman!

# Delayed Action

Lord,
Today I let my emotions
Become snarled
And tangled.
Let my nerves grow
Frayed and jangled...

Until I stopped
What I was doing
And found a quiet corner
For meditating.

Lord,
Why do I take so long,
When You are always there,
Waiting?

# Keeping My Cool

Lord,
When You were assembling
The various components
Which went into
My creation,
Why did You omit
Composure...
That inner serenity
Which would allow me
To react calmly to
Any given situation?

Was it because
Composure is something
You want me
Not only to learn
But earn?

# The Alien

Lord,
There is so much
In today's world that
I do not understand.

Offices are run by
Machines of which
I have never even heard.
The whole field of
High technology
Is totally beyond me,
The space program
Bewilders me.

I find myself wandering
In a wilderness of
Noncomprehension,
Surrounded by people
Speaking a foreign tongue.
Lord, I feel so dumb!
Who needs me?

I know, I know.
YOU need me,
Thank heaven!

# Plea

Lord,
Someone I love
Is hurting.
Someone I love
Is grappling with
Pain and shock.
Someone I love
Needs more help
Than I can give.

Lord,
Please surround her,
Enfold her, uphold her
With Your strength
And comfort.
Lord,
Help her to want
To live.

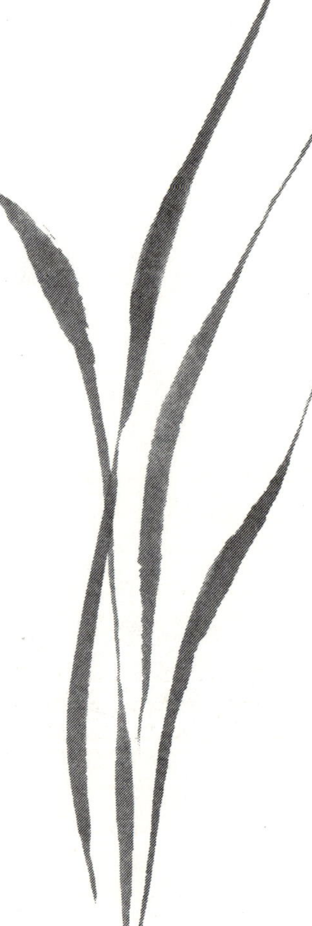

# Bottom Line

Lord,
Today I made such
A stupid mistake,
And I am so ashamed!
I disrupted a whole
Group of people,
Caused endless trouble,
Yet they were so
Kind and patient,
And I was not
Even blamed!

Lord,
I know THEY forgive me,
And YOU forgive me,
Now please help ME
To forgive me!

# Turning Point

Lord,
Today I left the house,
Wanting never to come back.
This nagging problem
Which does not go away
Grew too large,
Too hopeless;
I could not see
Around it,
Through it,
Or over it,
And I gave in
To despair.

But You met me
On the front walk,
And quietly asked me
To await Your will.
You put Your arm
Through mine,
Turned me around,
And led me gently
Back in, and now
I feel calm
And still.

Thank You, Lord,
For being there.

## House Beautiful

It is said
That a woman's home
Reflects her personality;
Her choice of colors
Reveals her emotional makeup;
The style of furniture
Tells volumes about
Her life-style.

Think of that!

When all I want
My home to do
Is show how much
This family
Loves You.

# Personal Achievement

Lord,
I did not address the U.N.
On world affairs today,
Or speak to a group of
Wall Street brokers;
Did not advise
Corporate lawyers on
Creative tax shelters,
Or chair a committee
On the changing role
Of women in industry...

But I did make
A coconut cream pie
Which held together for once
And did not have to be
Served as pudding...

And I did get to the
Library meeting on time
And even remembered
To bring the minutes...

And after supper
My good mate and I
Drove to the beach
To watch one of Your more
Spectacular sunsets.

What a super day
This has been, Lord!

## Along His Path

Lord,
Thank You again
For compensating for
My laggard feet.

I too often grow weary
And stop at the half-way mark,
But always You go
That extra mile,
So we can meet.

# Storm at Sea

Lord,
This has been
Such a long day.
It seems years
Since I awoke this morning,
Full of plans,
My schedule all
Mapped out.

One telephone call
Changed all that.
A schoolground accident,
Ambulance,
Hospital,
Doctors,
Discussions,
Decisions,
And the waiting...

Now at sunset,
I sink with gratitude
To my knees.
Tragedy has been averted,
Things are back on course,
And troubled waters
Are calm again,
All because
You were doing the
Navigating.

## Television Survey

Lord,
When I have a complaint,
I believe in going
Right to the top!

You see, the situation for women
Down here is really bleak,
When Monday night football
Goes on all week.

So I am asking, Lord,
If You could possibly arrange
For those ratings
To drop.

# Clearing the Decks

There are days
When I suspect my mind
Too much resembles
The interior of my purse...

A dark jungle
Cluttered with nonessentials,
Crumpled supermarket tapes,
Reminder notes for things
I forgot to do,
Empty gum wrappers
And a collection
Of odd cosmetics
Which do absolutely nothing
For me,
Beneath which important items,
Like wallet and keys,
Sink into oblivion and
Out of sight.

Lord,
Help me to clean out
Both my purse and my mind,
So that my priorities remain
Clearly before me,
Up front and
In the light.

# Renewal Project

Lord,
There is so much of me
That needs changing
If I am to become
The totally new person
I want to be,
Worthy of You.

Much of the old thinking
Needs to be torn out,
And there is extensive
Altering to do,
But I am eager to begin.

It will take awhile,
And we may have to
Start from the ground,
But the basic structure
Is sound,
Since You were the
Original architect...

And the wiring
Is already in.

# Message

Lord,
I know these words
Will never make
The best-seller list;
They will not go down
In history or be
Immortalized;
They are not profound
Or prophetic,
Certainly not in the least
Academic.

But Lord,
I will feel
So richly rewarded
If this small volume lights
Just one candle...
If just one reader
Might say,
"I want to know more
About this Lord
Of whom she writes!"